How to Start and Sustain a Faith-Based YOUNG ADULT GROUP

How to
Start and
Sustain a
Faith-Based
YOUNG
ADULT
GROUP

John D. Schroeder

ABINGDON PRESS / NASHVILLE

HOW TO START AND SUSTAIN A FAITH-BASED YOUNG ADULT GROUP

Library of Congress Cataloging-in-Publication Data

Schroeder, John D.
   How to start and sustain a faith-based young adult group / John D. Schroeder.
       p. cm.— (How to start—)
   ISBN 0-687-04619-X (pbk.: alk. paper)
   1. Church group work with young adults.   I. Title.   II. Series.
BV4446 .S37 2002
259'.25—dc21

                                                            2002007270

02 03 04 05 06 07 08 09 10 11—10 9 8 7 6 5 4 3 2 1

MANUFACTURED IN THE UNITED STATES OF AMERICA

CONTENTS

INTRODUCTION

The story is told of a farmer who sold his farm to go in search of diamonds. The man traveled all over the world and ended up broke and depressed. He eventually drowned himself in a river because his treasure had eluded him.

This tale did not end with the man's death, however. It seems that the man who purchased the farm was watering his livestock one day and discovered a glistening object in the stream. It was a diamond! His discovery led to virtually "acres of diamonds" on his property.

The young adults in your church and in your community are your very own "acres of diamonds." It is a ministry opportunity in your own backyard. These are people just starting out on their own, both married and single, who have great needs and great potential. They are high school and college graduates seeking answers to spiritual and secular issues.

A young adult ministry is an opportunity for shaping the spiritual development of those on their own for the first time. Some may be members of a church; others may not have any church background but now have an interest in developing the spiritual side of their lives. God is calling them to begin a relationship with Jesus Christ. Members of a young adult group minister to each other as they grow together in faith.

Young adult groups also offer a chance for social development. Social needs are met within a Christian atmosphere. Group activities offer an opportunity to develop new people skills. Friendships are born. Those who are lonely find they are not alone. Some are searching for a lifetime companion. Others want to be a part of a group of like-minded individuals who share common interests. All are searching for meaning and direction, longing to connect with God, others, and themselves.

Just like all people, each young adult group is unique. Every group will have different perspectives, dynamics, feelings, and adventures. The size of the group may be as small as five or number in the hundreds. Some groups gather weekly, others monthly. And activities will vary from small group discussions to a wide range of social events.

Love and acceptance is a vital aspect of this ministry. It's important that young adults be accepted just as they are. Each person will be on a different point on life's journey. Some will be believers, some nonbelievers, and some will be seekers. The only thing some may have in common will be their age group. Interests and occupations will vary. Each person, however, will have something valuable to contribute as a member of your young adult group.

This book is intended to be a road map for your journey, from conception to completion. Like all human beings, young adult groups are life-forms that are born, flourish, and eventually die. This book contains options and information to assist you on your journey. Remember that there are many roads that reach the same destination. As you begin your journey, there are many decisions to be made. This guide contains ideas and options. Use what you think will work best for you. Feel free to experiment.

Finally, since you are starting a faith-based group, use the power of prayer to guide you and your group toward the destination God has in mind for you. The journey will be one like you have never had before, and God will be with you every step of the way.

CHAPTER 1

Initial Decisions and Planning

Congratulations! You are about to experience the creation of a young adult group, a ready-made family of individuals who will touch one another's lives. As leader and organizer, you will need to make some decisions and do some planning in order to reach your objectives. Let's begin with your objectives.

Why do you want to start a young adult group?

A young adult group in your church should exist only to nurture the young adults in your midst. If your motivation is to love and care for young adults, you are on the right track.

Not every church should attempt to start a young adult group. Not every church has a ready population of young adults nor does every church have the time, patience, and leadership to develop a young adult ministry. Starting a young adult ministry will not necessarily bring new people into your congregation. It may not help your church grow.

Even if your heart and head are in the right places, it is not always easy to launch a young adult group. You will need to be able to interest enough young adults to allow the group to continue and be successful. A church starting a young adult group also needs a natural population of young adults in its vicinity.

Take a good look at the number of young adults who are related to your congregation and who live in your area. These persons represent your natural population of young adults. How many people are on your list? The best planned event will attract only 20 to 30 percent of the natural population. Will that number be enough to maintain interest and allow the group to continue? Some congregations find that cooperating with other nearby churches can help enlarge the natural population necessary for a continuing young adult group.

✳ Goals

If you believe that there are enough young adults around to make a young adult group possible, look at your objectives along with the needs of young adults. You want to start a group in which young adults can find space and support for their spiritual growth. Consider making a list of the goals or outcomes for the group and individual participants. Put your vision in writing.

Think about how you will meet the needs of those who will become members of your young adult group. It is important to remember that people join groups in order to have their needs met. They come to a group for a reason and with an agenda.

Participants also have different needs from one another. One person may join solely for friendship (to make new Christian friends) while another might attend in order to have his or her spiritual needs met. A young adult group can satisfy multiple needs, but these needs should be considered in your initial planning.

In considering needs, it is important to look at where young adults are at this point in their lives. Most young adults are at a stage where they have moved from their parents' households to college dorms, apartments, or houses of their own. They are becoming independent from their families and are on their own for the first time. They are becoming adults in their own right.

Young adults are dealing with many issues, including independence, identity, and intimacy. The loneliness of being on their own may cause them to yearn for new and intimate relationships. In addition, some may be starting their first jobs and are now responsible for paying rent, making car payments, and buying food, clothing, and furnishings for a home.

Young adult ministry provides opportunities for

persons to share their struggles. Young adults often seek a community of friends, peers, and mentors as they search for answers. They are looking for direction in both the secular and spiritual realms.

Young adults also have spiritual concerns. They are questioning, exploring, and experimenting. They have moved away from their parents and are beginning to make their own world of meanings. Some may leave the church during this time while others may attend Sunday worship on a regular basis.

It is normal for young adults to question matters of faith. When they do so, however, they do not necessarily reject the faith of their parents. If young adults reject anything at this point, they reject a naïve acceptance of parental authority as the guarantee of faith. Young adults need to "own" their understandings of faith. And so they question.

The best responses that older adults and friends of young adults can have are to accept the questioning of young adults, to accept their questions, to allow them to try answers of their own without condemnation, and to model with integrity and consistency their own set of faith understandings.

✳ Participants

Once you have some idea why you want to form a young adult group and have thought about their needs and how you might meet them, it is time to make some decisions about your prospective participants. One decision is the number of participants to have.

There are several factors to consider when determining the size of your young adult group. First, you will want to look at the amount of space available. Are you planning to have your activities in a large room, small room, gymnasium, or outdoors? Will the young adults need space on Sunday mornings, or will they be meeting on a weekday evening?

You may want the group to be small enough so everyone gets a chance to participate, especially if you are having a Bible study or small group discussion. One option is to break down a large group into a number of small groups for some events. Remember that some people will be absent from time to time. Think about seating, comfort, and the ability to hear each other.

Many young adult groups have no restrictions as to the number of people. They welcome and accommodate everyone who shows up. These groups have both large and small group activities when they get together. Gymnasiums and large and small rooms within churches are often used.

The type of people is another consideration. Is your young adult group open to singles, married, or both? Will participants be solely members of your church, people from the neighborhood, or anyone who wants to attend? And there is also the question of what age group constitutes a young adult. Normally, young adults are ages 18 to 39. Some groups could be composed of men and women in their twenties. It is important to establish an age range early in the planning process.

✳ Research

The next step in the creation of your young adult group should be some research that can add to your potential for a successful ministry. Using your list of potential members, conduct some personal interviews. Get to know your potential group members. Meet them face-to-face. Learn about their situations, their interests, and their needs. This is your opportunity to become an "expert" on young adults.

Prepare some appropriate questions in advance concerning their needs, interests, and ideas on scheduling events. Ask them if they think they would participate in a new young adult group. What would they like the group to do? Give them some possible activities as examples. Would they be willing to attend on Sunday mornings during the Sunday school hour? Would they prefer a weekend? What time is best? You might also ask them if they know other young adults who would be interested in this new group.

Interview as many young adults as possible, then sit down and review your findings. Learn from what you were told. What programming received the most positive response? Were they interested in attending on Sunday mornings or on a weeknight? Would they invest one, two, or three hours of their time on a weekly or monthly basis?

✳ Leadership Options

Now that you are ready to make some initial decisions, it is time to focus on the question of leadership. You have several options open to you including a single leader or a leadership team. Consider the qualities you are looking for in a leader.

You want a person who relates well to young adults and has a knack for young adult ministry. One of the most important traits of a young adult leader is to be a good listener. Young adults need accepting, patient people to hear them out. You want someone who can invest the time to launch a program and then do what is necessary to keep it operating. If the group will be meeting weekly, a leader's schedule must be free so he or she can be there each week. Another quality needed in a leader is creativity. Are they able to conceive and sustain activities that keep the interest and meet the needs of young adults? A leader also needs good organizational ability. This is the ability to delegate or handle a multitude of tasks, making sure all the details get covered. You also want a leader who is reliable to do the work necessary while being responsive to the needs of the group.

Group leadership involves a number of responsibilities. Beyond the tasks involved in starting a group, a leader is often the facilitator of each meeting and each small group session. The leader also keeps track of individual members. Small group members may call the leader if they are unable to attend. The leader is responsible for notifying members if a meeting is canceled. Some responsibilities of the leader can certainly be delegated.

The leader is the shepherd of the group, looking out for his or her flock. If problems develop within the group, the group leader deals with them. If a small group discussion is offered, lesson preparation is involved each week as well as any after-discussion group activities or social events.

Another duty of the leader is to initially decide where and when to meet. Normally, a young adult group meets at a church, but some meet in the homes of members or in rooms at public libraries or restaurants.

The criteria for deciding on a location include lighting, size of the group, comfortable seating, privacy, and closeness to the members' homes. Availability of the proposed location is a first concern. Is there available parking, and is it in a safe area of town? The leader also needs to check that there are no scheduling conflicts with other groups for the facility.

Taking all of the above into consideration, the question becomes can one person fulfill all of these traits, or is a leadership team required? Here are a few options to consider:

- The leader could be the youth pastor of the church.
- A seminary student could be utilized in the role of leader, either as an internship or on a salary basis.
- The leader could be a member of the congregation who has the time and interest to coordinate a young adult ministry.

Another option is to set up a leadership team if you are older than the young adults you are leading. Young adults want to take part in making decisions that affect them. If you are a young adult yourself, set up a leadership team anyway. The diversity present in a group of three to five will add knowledge and skills to what you offer as an individual.

If you are responsible for establishing a leadership team, recruit carefully. Do not simply ask for volunteers. You could end up with a group of persons who lack the combination of skills required to meet the demands of a young adult ministry.

✳ Costs and Funding

It doesn't take much money to start a young adult group. The only costs involved would be for a text for small group discussions, costs for promoting the group, snacks, and supplies for activities, such as volleyball equipment. If the leader is being paid for his or her time, that would be an added expense.

Normally the cost of the materials, such as a textbook for group discussions, would be covered by each of the participants. Refreshments could be a shared expense by members of the group with each person taking turns bringing a snack for the week. The cost of other items would need to come from the church budget, or perhaps a member of the congregation would donate funds.

Another alternative for funding and meeting the needs of the group could be to seek donations from local businesses. A business owned by a member of the congregation might donate the cost of pizza for a special event. A business might sponsor your softball, bowling, or volleyball team.

✳ Scheduling

When scheduling your initial programming, it pays to ask your prospective members for their advice. Many weeknight groups begin at 7:00 or 7:30, allowing people to get home from work, eat, and get to church. Some groups run activities from 7:00 to 9:00 P.M. Ask your members for their input on when to conclude activities.

Ask for suggestions on what night is best. Many churches have Wednesday night or Thursday night activities for all members of the church. Is there space to accommodate a young adult group with other groups? Other churches have young adult activities on Sunday mornings or Sunday nights. Take a good look at all your options. If it doesn't work, change to another day or time.

The other scheduling decision is which activity to schedule first. If you have only one activity, such as a Bible study, there is no decision to be made. However, more than one activity creates questions. Do you have a Bible study followed by volleyball, or volleyball followed by a small group discussion? Look at all your options and weigh the benefits of each.

CHAPTER 2

Activities and Options

After making some initial decisions about a young adult ministry and obtaining some feedback from prospective participants about their interests and needs, you should have some idea about what type of activities and programming you intend to offer.

There is a full range of options available to you from a weekly one-hour informal discussion on young adult issues to small group discussions, Bible studies, recreational activities, social events, special events, and retreats. You can offer as little or as much as you want. Your selection of programming will be determined by your number of participants, available space in your facility, the needs and interests of your young adults, and finally, how much time the leader has to invest in this ministry.

Programming may seek to meet the spiritual, social, or recreational needs of your group, but not necessarily all three. Again, it depends on the needs and interests of your young adults. It is wise to listen to your prospective group members before making any decisions. You can also be experimental in your programming, keeping what works and changing what doesn't. There may be a period of trial and error for up to a year before you find programming that meets needs and generates attendance.

✳ Quality Programs

Young adults choose the activities in which they want to take part. If they do not find an activity worthwhile, they will not come back. Quality is essential. When starting out, it is vital to be organized, have the necessary materials in place to offer a program, and offer a welcoming and accepting atmosphere.

You should also think about the activities against which your young adult group competes. Your competition could include everything from staying home and watching television to going out to a play, movie, or restaurant. One major plus you have going for you is that attending your young adult group will be cheaper than going to a movie or out to dinner. Money does matter. Some times, even the weather will be a factor and compete against you.

In the end, however, the question remains, *what would cause the persons you hope to attract to choose your group instead of some other activity?*

If your group meets on Sunday morning, how can you help young adults choose to get up early enough to attend instead of sleeping late? When you invite young adults, you are asking them to give up some of their limited free time. What will be in it for them to be there on Sunday morning or to drop by church on a Wednesday night after a hard day of work?

Preparation pays big dividends. The more preparation you do, the easier it will be for you to get your group off the ground. Do your homework. If you are leading a session, prepare well in advance. Have adequate copies of materials available. If you are unsure how to carry out an activity, try it out on family members or friends.

Pay attention to your meeting room. Some of your young adults will be brand new to the congregation. Look at your meeting room as if you were seeing it for the first time. What is your first impression? What can you change to make it more inviting? Can a new person find it easily? How can a young adult coming into the church for the first time know that a group of persons of his or her age is meeting in your room? If you want young adults who are parents to come, child care is another issue. Will you offer quality day care, or do they need to make their own arrangements?

If leaders of young adults should cultivate any one virtue, it is hospitality. Create a safe, inviting environment for the members of your group. Offer an oasis in the midst of a shifting, uncertain life. Provide more than you promise.

Think of it this way: Many young adults might recently have left the home of their parents to live on their own for the first time. Many of them have moved to new communities. They find themselves living among strangers. They need to belong. Where better to belong than a church's young adult group?

If you are the leader, think of those who attend your programming as guests. What can you do to make them feel more comfortable? How can you welcome them? How can you make them feel welcome and that they belong here? How might you refresh them? And most important, how can you be sure that when they leave, they will be looking forward to the time they can return?

✳ Small Group Meetings

Most young adult groups offer small group discussions or Bible studies to meet the spiritual needs of participants. These might be on Sunday morning between worship services or on a weekday evening, often in conjunction with other young adult activities. Chances are you have participated in or perhaps led a small group discussion in the past. Here are some of the basics:

People helping people grow in faith is the ministry of the small group. A small group is usually a group of twelve or fewer who gather together on a regular basis to study God's word and encourage each other in faith. It is people ministering to each other. Just as Jesus used his twelve disciples to change the world, God can use small groups to change lives. It is a vital aspect of your young adult ministry.

Small groups are an opportunity for individuals to discuss issues of faith in a nonthreatening and supportive environment. It is a place for young adults to ask questions and learn from one another. In small groups, members learn from one another as ideas and experiences are shared.

In preparing to launch your small group for young adults, you need to consider a number of aspects about meetings. In most cases, the number of times your small group will meet will be decided by your choice of topic and material. If the book you selected has twelve chapters, that pretty much determines the number of meetings. You would meet for twelve weeks, and then go on to another book, with or without a break.

Another idea is to have an "open" small group with a different topic each time using the Bible as a text. The leader would create a topic and discussion questions. Anyone could show up and join the discussion. There would be no participant preparation needed nor any strict attendance requirements. People would attend as they are able. For example, it could be promoted that your church has a young adult small group that meets each Tuesday night at seven for ninety minutes, and all are welcome.

The traditional alternative is to have a small group that meets weekly for a set number of weeks (determined by the number of chapters in a book) with the same participants each week. Each member would own a copy of the book, read the lesson each week, and come prepared to discuss it. This format does make it difficult to add new participants weeks into the discussion. It also obligates the members to make a commitment to attend each week in order to have enough people for a lively discussion. Can you get your young adults to make this commitment?

The length of each session for many small groups is from one hour to ninety minutes. You want to allow enough time for social time, topic discussion, and perhaps an activity. This would be in addition to any time spent for a large group activity or recreational activity. Most participants find they can spare an hour a week, plus travel time to and from the discussion location. You want to allow enough time to complete your small group discussion while respecting individual time restrictions.

It is important to note that perhaps not all your young adults will want to attend the small group discussion, but they may be interested in the activity that comes before or after the discussion. Some young adult groups offer volleyball or softball followed by a small group Bible study. Flexible scheduling helps you meet the needs and interests of your young adults.

✳ Discussion Materials

When it comes to discussion material for your small group, there are thousands of options. You may already know exactly the text you want to use, and if so, you can move on to other decisions. If you are undecided, two options are using a Christian-theme book or the Bible for your discussion. Your local Christian bookstore or your church library can provide many ideas and options. You can also use the Internet to explore potential material.

Here are some idea starters:

- The basics of Christianity
- Learning your identity as a Christian

- Gaining spiritual maturity
- Living as a Christian
- The power of the Lord's Prayer
- Living a life of faith in a secular world
- Learning about Christ's twelve apostles

If you are planning a small group Bible study, there are a few things to keep in mind. All participants should be using the same version of the Bible. The leader should determine the version, perhaps with input from participants. You could ask what version they own and go with the majority, if you desire.

Your local bookstore is an excellent source for locating discussion guides for various books of the Bible. Discussion guides contain questions for the group to answer and sometimes they include group activities. Your first step is to select which book of the Bible you want to study. Discussion guides exist for most books. You will want to select a guide that is compatible with your beliefs and your denomination. Look at how many weeks or sessions the guide is divided into, and compare the costs. You also need to decide if you want to purchase just one study guide for the leader, or if you want each member to have a guide and access to the weekly questions. Your pastor may also have suggestions on which study guide to use.

If you want to use a Christian-themed book, there are many to choose from. Again, your church library and your local Christian bookstore are great places to begin your search. Many Christian publishers, such as Abingdon Press, are now including study guides in the backs of books. Separate companion study guides for Christian books are also available from many publishers. Many books are located in the inspirational or Christian Living sections of bookstores.

Not all books come with a study guide containing questions for a group discussion. Having a ready-made study guide does make it easier for the discussion leader, but you can lead a discussion without one. In such a case, the leader and/or participants would be responsible for coming up with questions.

Another option is to study a secular book and focus on how it relates to your Christian faith. For example, a book on job hunting could be used for a small group if many of your young adults are looking for work. Topics for each session could include prayer, networking with other Christians, contacts within the church, trusting in God, and other related themes. Another example is a secular book on gardening with homemade questions on spiritual themes such as faith, spiritual nourishment, and planting seeds. Verses from the Bible could serve as themes.

Take care in selecting a book. Your choice can affect the quality of the discussions. You want to look for a subject that will hold the interest of your small group for the duration of the class. You may want to read the book in its entirety first before the group starts to determine if you can live with it for several months.

Consider if the text would encourage good discussion. Is it suited for young adults? Does it contain stories that illustrate Christian themes? Is it easy to read or quite dry? And finally, ask yourself if this is a book that is worth the time that will be invested. Consider whether your participants will gain spiritual growth as a result of reading this book. You might take one or more members of your young adult group along when you look at books. Consider their opinions on topics and books.

Remember that the book you select is a catalyst for God to work within your group. Much of the spiritual growth may come from the discussions and from members ministering to one another.

✳ Recreational Options

While some young adult groups are built solely around a small group discussion or Bible study, other small groups include a recreational activity before or after the small group session. The recreational activity may be weekly or once a month as a special event.

Recreational activities are often included in programming to offer variety. While a Bible study may not appeal to all young adults, an occasional volleyball or softball game might generate attendance. Sometimes people might come for the recreation and then decide to stay for the small group. Some athletic activity is also very appealing to those who sit at a desk all day at work.

If your church has a gymnasium, you have an advantage when it comes to recreational programming. Activities like basketball and volleyball can be scheduled on a regular basis. If your church does not have a gym, check with neighboring churches and schools.

Some recreational programming options for your young adult group include: volleyball, bowling, softball, basketball, swimming, miniature golf, soccer, badminton, and tennis. Most of these sports do require equipment that could be obtained from members of the group or purchased by a sponsoring local business. If your church has a gym, chances are they also have equipment for gym sports.

A number of these activities are outdoor sports that can be played at a nearby park during the spring, summer, and fall. Volleyball and basketball can move into a gym during the winter. Most sports are inexpensive, which is another plus for health-conscious young adults.

If you do offer a recreational event, check with your church about their liability insurance coverage.

✳ Social Opportunities

Many young adult groups offer a monthly social event where members can become better acquainted and deepen their friendships. These events can be scheduled, planned, and implemented by the leader or by volunteers from the group. The scheduled social event should be announced weeks in advance so everyone knows about it. Some groups schedule a social event for a certain day each month, such as every third Saturday, so members can pencil it in on their calendars.

The best part about having a social event is that it can be as simple or as elaborate as you wish. The cost is usually minimal and some events require no cost, such as board games at the church or at a member's house. You can be as creative as you want. And with such a variety of options available, your young adults need never be bored with the same old thing.

Some popular options are:

- See movies—go to the local movie theater as a group.
- Play board games—members bring their favorite board games to church or to the home of a member.
- Watch videos—watch a video at church or at the home of a member. Perhaps have a discussion about it later.
- Go out to eat—take the gang out for pizza.
- Fly a kite—can be done any time of the year as long as there is wind.
- Play cards—get a few decks of cards and have some fun.
- See a play—catch a show at the local playhouse.
- Go roller skating, ice skating, roller blading— all are great exercise.
- Have seasonal parties—for Valentine's Day, Christmas, New Year's.
- Take in a sports event—see the local professional sports team in action, or watch a high school or college game.
- Have a hobby night—show-and-tell time about your hobby.
- Throw a painting party—hand out paint, brushes, and boards. See who can create a masterpiece!

These are just a few of the things you can do as a group that will help you get to know one another better at the same time. Some events may require a carpool, while others can take place on church property. Ask your young adults for suggestions about what they want to do.

✳ Special Events

In addition to recreational and social events, some young adult groups also schedule special events. These are once-a-year activities that become a tradition and are highly anticipated. Your creativity plays a major role here.

For example, one young adult group has a miniature golf tournament in August of every year. The winner receives a huge trophy that is theirs to keep until next year. Everyone goes out for pizza with the winner. Another special event could be a Young Adult Olympics. These events could include:

- Balloon Volleyball—Divide participants into two teams. A low sheet or net separates them. The players either sit on chairs or on the floor. A balloon is used as the volleyball and is hit back and forth over the net by the two teams. A point is scored when the balloon touches the ground. The first team to score ten points is the winner.

- Drop-it, a guessing game—All you need to do is stand behind a sheet and drop objects on the floor while participants guess what was dropped. They write down their guesses on a sheet of paper. Use about 15 common items such as a golf ball, a dime, a pencil, a piece of wood, a book, and a spoon. The person who correctly guesses the most items wins.
- Tissue racing—Tissue racing is a relay race with tissue paper carried on a tablespoon. The tissue paper is about two inches square and sits on a pillow at one end of the room. It gets carried on a tablespoon across the room to a coffee cup, which sits on a table. The tissue must not be touched by anything. If it falls off, the tissue must be picked up by the spoon. Two teams compete.

Be creative. Add some more events to the above list and you have yourself a Young Adult Olympics! Get some trophies or ribbons to give to the winners.

CHAPTER 3

The First Meeting

Once you have decided on which activities to offer and when to offer them, you are ready to begin your young adult group. Your next step is to publicize your young adult group and plan for your first gathering.

Set a goal of how many young adults you want to attend. If you are having just one small group, you probably only want six to twelve people to accept your invitation. If you have other activities planned and can accommodate more, invite more. Getting a firm commitment to attend is a plus. Personal invitations are the best way to encourage young adults to attend your opening session. Using your entire list of prospects, make recruitment personal. Telephone them. Email them. Visit them. Write them notes. Offer them rides.

Publicize the start of your new group in whatever media might be available. Announce it during worship. Get it in the church bulletin and the monthly church newsletter. Focus, however, on creating excitement by word of mouth. Be sure to encourage those you invite to bring a friend along. This can not only increase the number of people attending the first session but also make those attending more comfortable because they will know at least one other young adult.

You also might want to phone or email each person prior to the meeting to remind them of the meeting and the starting time. A telephone call provides the opportunity to get to know them a bit better, and you can answer any questions they have.

✳ First Meeting Guide

This next section is intended to guide you through your first session. You'll probably be both excited and nervous the day or evening of your first small group meeting. You are about to begin a valuable ministry that can make an impression on your young adults for years to come. Share with God in prayer your feelings and ask for guidance as you get ready to lead your first session.

Before you begin, remember that this meeting will probably serve just two purposes. First, people will have time to get to know one another. Second, it will be a time for you to provide basic information to them and answer any questions. There may not be enough time for discussion of the first lesson. You could use the time to hand out a copy of the book you will be using and give an overview. Remember the importance of making a good first impression. Make the first session festive. Have fun. Provide a balance of fellowship and study time. It's best to arrive early at the location of your meeting so you can welcome all the participants and make introductions. Chances are you and your participants may not know everyone there. Try some icebreakers to get your members to mingle and become comfortable with one another.

Some icebreaker ideas:

- Give each person a sheet of paper and a pen as he or she enters. Ask them to get the autographs of all the other people.
- Have each person share his or her favorite place, favorite person, and favorite pastime, recreation, or hobby. Since the first person sets the tone, select someone who feels comfortable sharing with others. Encourage people to say as little or as much as they feel comfortable sharing with the group.
- As people enter the room, give each a card with the name of half a common pair written on it. Examples: *Adam* and *Eve*, *Jack* and *Jill*, *Salt* and *Pepper*. *Salt* would be on one card while *Pepper* would be on another. Ask each

person to match the pair before the meeting starts.

- Break the group into pairs and have each person interview their partner for five minutes. Information such as name, family, occupation, and hobbies may be shared. After the interviews are completed, each person introduces his or her partner to the rest of the group.

- Ask participants to mingle and discover a common bond with each of the other people. It may be wearing the same pair of shoes, being born in the same month or city, or having graduated from the same school. Have them report their common bonds to the group prior to the meeting.

Use your own imagination to think up other ways to get people talking to one another. You may want to have an icebreaker at the start of both the first and second sessions. Depending on the size of your group, you may want to give each person a name tag for this first meeting.

After the icebreaker, get your group seated. Start on time. Welcome them. Share your enthusiasm for this opportunity. Introduce the book you will be studying. You may want to cover why this book was selected and give an overview. Also, share what you want to accomplish as a young adult group. Ask participants to briefly talk about why they decided to attend and what they expect to receive and learn.

Review the format for future meetings and tell them how much time will be spent on each segment. For example:

1. Social time
2. Check-in, where each person reports how they are, what's new since last week, and so forth
3. Announcements by the leader
4. Book discussion (which can be followed by a group activity)
5. Closing prayer
6. Refreshments, social time

If you have planned for and have time for discussion, go ahead. Following are some suggestions for the leader on how to facilitate the discussion.

✳ Leader Guidelines

1. Know your people. Good teachers know that they teach persons, not lessons.

2. Avoid controlling the group. One of the most common mistakes a leader makes is to try to control what happens in the group. The group as a whole is responsible for what takes place during the session itself.

3. Keep aware of what is going on in the group. How are individuals responding and interacting? Is discussion lagging due to lack of interest? Do you

need to allow more time for an activity that is going well? You want to remain flexible.

4. Prior to the meeting, read the chapter and highlight important sentences or paragraphs. Make notes in the margins if you desire. Get comfortable with the material.

5. If your book contains questions or comes with a study guide that contains questions, review them in advance. Remember, you don't have to use all the questions in the study guide, and you can create your own.

6. If your book does not contain discussion questions, you can write your own. Jot down questions as they come to you while reading the lesson. You may want to begin group discussion with a general question each week such as *What new insights did you receive from reading this chapter?* You can also ask group members to begin the discussion with their own questions or a topic they want to discuss. (All the questions do not have to come from you.) You can write questions about the meanings of words. Ask members to talk about a personal experience with the topic of the session. One way to conclude discussion is by asking a general question such as *How has this discussion helped or challenged you?* Try to prepare about a dozen questions for each chapter.

7. For the first couple of sessions, you may want to begin by reminding participants that not every-

one may feel comfortable reading aloud, answering questions, or participating in group activities. Encourage them to participate as they feel comfortable doing so.

8. You could begin discussion by reviewing the main points of the chapter and providing the group with a summary. You may ask group members what they saw as highlights.

9. Encourage questions. Remind your participants that all questions are valid as part of the learning process. When you ask questions, you give permission for people to talk to others, exchanging thoughts and feelings.

10. Even if people don't talk during a discussion, you can be assured there is an internal dialogue enabling people to get in touch with their feelings.

11. Some questions may be more difficult to answer than others. If you ask a question and no one responds, begin the discussion by venturing an answer yourself. Then ask for comments and other answers. Remember that some questions may have multiple answers.

12. Ask the questions "Why?" or "Why do you believe that?" to help continue a discussion and give it greater depth.

13. Give everyone a chance to talk. Keep the conversation moving. Occasionally you may want to direct a question to a specific person who has

been quiet. "Do you have anything to add?" is a good follow-up question to another person. If the conversation gets off track, move ahead by asking the next question.

14. Before moving from questions to activities, ask group members if they have any questions that have not been answered.

15. Remember that as a leader, you do not have to know all the answers. Some answers may come from group members. Other answers may even need a bit of research. Your job is to keep the discussion moving and to encourage participation.

16. Be grateful and supportive. Thank group members for their ideas and participation.

17. You are not expected to be a "perfect" leader. Just do the best you can by focusing on the participants and the lesson. God will help you lead this group. Enjoy your time together.

✳ Group Guidelines

Explain that this group is a family and has some ground rules for the benefit of the entire family. These rules include:

1. *Confidentiality.* What is said within the group stays within the group. Do not share personal information from this group with friends or your family. This is a safe place to talk.

2. *Purpose.* This is not a therapy group, a sensitivity group, or an encounter group. We are here to grow in faith and closer to God. We can offer Christian love and support to one another.

3. *Schedule.* Each session will start on time and end on time. Please be prompt. Let someone know if you are unable to attend.

4. *Equality.* All are equals. No one is expected to be an expert on a topic.

5. *Acceptance.* It is important that each person be accepted by the rest of the group just as they are. We are all members of the family of God.

✳ Participant Guidelines

1. What you will receive from this study will be in direct proportion to your involvement. Feel free to share your thoughts about the material being discussed. Participate as your comfort level permits.

2. Please be supportive and encourage your fellow participants.

3. Please read the lesson and review the questions prior to the meeting. You may want to jot down answers to some of the questions.

4. You may be unable to answer some of the discussion questions. This is not a problem. No one has all the answers. Any ventured answer or guess is welcome.

5. There may be more than one answer to some questions.

6. Pray for your group and your leader.

Once you have reviewed the basics, you may or may not have time for discussion of the first lesson. If you have not done so already, you could distribute books and talk about the book. This is also a good time to solicit questions from your group members. You could also end the meeting with more social time or another icebreaker.

✳ Group Activities

Discussion questions can be followed by a group activity. An activity is an excellent way to encourage group interaction and sharing of ideas and information. They can add depth to the topic being discussed. Here are some suggestions about planning an activity.

1. Some study guides include multiple suggestions for activities. This gives you the option of selecting which idea is best suited for your group. If you are not using a study guide, you or a group member can create your own activity. You'll want to set aside a specific amount of time for this event.

2. Select your activity in advance and plan for it. If the activity requires pens and paper, be sure you

bring them along. Drawing or creating something could be a group activity.

3. Your activity could be a group discussion on a specific topic. It might be creating a list of some sort related to your topic. If you come up with a hot question that lends itself toward a lengthy discussion, use it in the activity section of your meeting.

4. Your activity could be watching a movie or video, followed by a brief group discussion.

5. Some groups use the Bible as a resource after completing discussion questions to delve into a specific aspect of a topic.

6. Magazines and newspapers are often used in an activity to search for local or national connections to a topic.

7. Try a field trip as an activity sometime over the course of your sessions. For example, if the topic is death or dying, a visit to a local cemetery or funeral home could be beneficial.

8. A practical application to what you are studying can become an excellent group activity. Visiting a nursing home as a group is a practical application for the topic of loneliness. Community service projects are also avenues to apply what you have been studying.

9. An activity could be a practical application after your meeting is over. It might be as simple as asking each member to share what they learned from this lesson with a family member or friend.

10. A challenge for the coming week could serve as an activity. For example, if the topic is kindness, the challenge could be to perform an act of kindness this week involving a total stranger. Members could report results at the next session.

CHAPTER 4

Long-Term Goals

God cares for people through people. This is how your young adult group will be sustained, as people minister to one another. As leader, you can't sustain and nurture your group alone. It is a group effort by you, your members, and God working together.

First, remember that your group is faith based. Your faith and the faith of your members are how God works within your young adult group. Prayer is one of the most important elements of sustaining a group. Your prayers, along with the prayers of your members, can work wonders in changing lives and drawing people closer to God. Prayer brings God in as an active participant in your young adult group. Pray for your group and encourage members to do the same. This will help sustain your group.

Second, remember the importance of being a good listener. Sometimes this involves listening to what is being said as well as to what is not. Listening can be just as vital to sustaining your group as words and actions. Listen for signs of people reaching out to others for help or needs not being met. Keeping your ears open is an excellent way to keep an accurate sense of your members. Remind your participants of the importance of being good listeners.

Third, encourage members to minister to each other. This ministry can take many forms. It can be as simple as phoning someone during the week to see how they are doing or having a cup of coffee with a member after the meeting ends. Sharing your faith with one member or the entire group is a wonderful ministry. It all comes down to showing you care and putting your faith into action. Again, your small group is not a therapy group, and members need to understand the difference. However, showing love and concern for others is what God wants us to do, and this will sustain your young adult group.

Finally, remain receptive to God's Spirit. God does work in mysterious ways to bring healing and to change lives. Seeds may be planted in your group that will blossom years later. Your group will be sustained by God, and you simply have to trust in that. You were all brought together by God for a purpose. Let God's Spirit lead and sustain your ministry.

✳ **Providing More Than You Promise**

It is the little things that count. Sustaining your young adult group is often a matter of being thoughtful and making that extra effort to minister to members of the group. The more you can encourage your group to become a family, the healthier you group will be.

Creating a weekly or monthly newsletter about your group is one special touch that pays big dividends. It doesn't need to be anything fancy or elaborate. One side of a sheet of paper will do. You can include a listing of upcoming events, a welcome to new members, personal news about members such as who just got a new job or new car, birthday greetings, and any other information you deem appropriate. No postage is needed as they can be handed out at meetings and posted on bulletin boards. Give a copy to the pastor and church council members to keep them informed.

Remembering and celebrating the birthdays of members as a group is a thoughtful touch. It can be as simple as singing "Happy Birthday" as a group or passing around a card to sign.

Encourage the deepening of friendships and networking by creating a master list of member names and telephone numbers so people can keep in contact during the week. Include email addresses. Update and distribute monthly or as needed.

Helping one another creates "family" and "community" within your group. One opportunity to deepen relationships is to encourage members to be of service to one another. Getting a group together to help a member move his or her belongings from one place to another can create bonding and is always appreciated by the person who is moving.

✳ Growing Your Group

Sustaining your group means growing your young adult group by welcoming new people each month. It's inevitable that some members of your group will move out of the area or drop out due to scheduling conflicts. How do you attract new people to your group?

The best way to attract new young adults is to encourage your members to invite and bring their friends to a meeting. Personal invitations get results because they reduce the risk in joining a strange group. People are less likely to show up if they do not know anyone. They are more likely to show up accompanied by a group member who can provide "security" and introduce the new person to others.

The leader can also "grow the group" by maintaining and nurturing that initial list of prospective members that have not yet made it to a meeting. A telephone call or email to someone who was "busy" when the group was being formed may now find that person receptive. All it may take is a personal invitation from the leader or a member.

Leaders and members alike need to always be aware of how difficult it can be to walk into a room of people where you do not know anyone. Young adults who attend a meeting for the first time need to be welcomed and to feel welcome. You get one chance to make a first impression.

Follow-up is also important. When a new person shows up for the first time, it is to your advantage to get their telephone number so you can stay in contact. A few days after the meeting, the leader can phone them and see how things are going. All people are flattered that someone cares enough to remember them and call to talk.

Be aware that some first-timers will not come back a second time. It may or may not be anything you or the group did or did not do. Perhaps they just didn't click with the group, or they didn't find what they were seeking. If you did your best in welcoming them, you have nothing to regret.

A word of warning: Do not fall into the trap of judging the success of your group by the number of people who attend. A group of five young adults is just as valuable to God as a group of ten or twenty.

✳ Planning Retreats

Some young adult groups offer seasonal retreats. It's an excellent opportunity for group members to strengthen their bonds of friendship and grow spiritually. Usually the retreat runs from Friday night to Sunday afternoon. Locations can include a cabin of a member, a church camp, a state park, or a ski lodge.

The leader or a leadership team can select the location and plan the activities. The retreat can have a theme, if you desire. Transportation is by carpool with drivers being reimbursed for gas. Activities can be a mix of spiritual, recreational, and social events. Meals and snacks need to be well planned in advance.

The cost per person is determined by the leader or planning committee once all costs have been considered. Asking for a commitment and a deposit weeks in advance is wise. Set a firm deadline for registrations. Some churches offer scholarships for retreats for low income people.

Encourage members to take along their camera and to take lots of photographs. After the retreat, create a photo display at the church so church members can become better acquainted with the group. The display can also serve as a way of attracting new members.

✳ Performing Community Service

Young adult groups are at their best when they serve others. Service projects and fund-raisers are one way groups can contribute to their church and community. In return, young adults receive appreciation and the knowledge that they made a difference by giving of their time and talent.

Community service projects and fund-raisers can be conducted any time of the year. All that is required is a commitment from group members to give of their time and talent. Ideas for projects can come from the leader, young adult members, and church pastors. There are a multitude of needs in every community, so it should not be difficult to find a project that matches the talents of the group.

One common community service project is to paint the interior or exterior of a senior citizen's home. Often the recipient will furnish the paint and food in exchange for the painting. For groups in northern climates, raking leaves in the fall in the yards of senior citizens is another appreciated service.

If your young adult group plays volleyball or basketball, you could have a marathon fund-raiser for local charities. Young adults solicit pledges from family, friends, and church members. Often local businesses will sponsor the marathon and provide pizza and soft drinks.

✳ **Solving Problems**

There may be bumps in the road on your journey. As in life, not everything goes the way you plan or would want it to be. You may need to adjust your original expectations and goals. God may be taking your group in another direction that is different from the path you intended to take. So, what should you do if your group just does not seem to be working out?

First, figure out what is going on. Doing an evaluation may help. If you make the effort to observe and listen to your group, you may be able to anticipate and head off many potential problems.

Second, if the problem is in your small group discussions, remember that the life span of a small group is a relatively brief time—six to eight weeks normally. Most small groups will not have the chance to gel much in such a short period of time. Do not expect the kind of group development you might look for in a group that has lived together and shared together for years.

Third, keep in mind that although you are a leader, the main responsibility for how the group develops belongs to the group itself. You do the best you can to create a hospitable setting for your group's interactions. You do your homework to keep the discussion and interactions flowing. But ultimately, every member of the group individually and corporately bears responsibility for whatever happens within the life of the small group.

However, if any specific problems do show up, try these suggestions:

If new people feel uncomfortable or unwelcome, the problem and solution belong to your entire group. Established young adult groups that are on-going without any ending date may get too comfortable with the "regulars" and develop into cliques. This is normal. The problem starts when a new person shows up and feels like an outsider.

First, it is normal for a new person to feel like an outsider. They don't know anyone. New people are obligated to make an extra effort to become part of the group, Second, your group members need to be reminded to be sensitive to the needs of new people. "Regulars" need to go out of their way to talk to and include new people. As a leader, you can be a role model by being the first to welcome new people and by introducing them to each member of the group.

If one member dominates the group or small group discussions, help the group identify this problem for itself by asking group members to rate overall participation. In other words, get a discussion going about how your discussions and activities are going. Another option is to ask a discussion question with the request that each person respond briefly. As a leader, you can also practice gate-keeping during group discussions by saying, "We've heard from Joe; now what does someone else think?" If the problem becomes troublesome, speak gently outside of a group session with the member who dominates.

If one member is reluctant to participate in a discussion, ask each member to respond briefly to a discussion question in a round-robin fashion. Another option is to ask a reluctant participant what he or she thinks of a topic or question. You can also increase participation by dividing the larger group into smaller groups of two or three persons.

If your group strays from the topic during a discussion, judge whether the group has a legitimate reason for straying. By straying from your agenda, is the group setting an agenda more valid for their needs? Another option is to simply restate the original topic or question. If one individual keeps causing the group to stray inappropriately from the topic, speak to him or her outside of a session.

If someone drops out of the group, it might be because his or her needs are not being met within the group. You will never know unless you ask that person directly. You should contact a person immediately following a first unplanned absence. Otherwise, they are unlikely to return.

If someone shares a big, dangerous, or bizarre problem, remember your young adult group is not a therapy group. You should not take on the responsibility of "fixing" someone else's problem. You should encourage a member who shares a major problem to seek professional help. If necessary, remind the group about the need for confidentiality. If someone shares something that endangers either himself or herself or someone else, contact your pastor for advice.

✳ Evaluating

How do you know if your young adult group is healthy? In order to sustain your group, some regular evaluation is smart. As a leader, your observations, which can often be based on your feelings, are important. You should also evaluate with input from participants. You may want to evaluate your group after several meetings rather than waiting toward the end. Here are some ideas on how to evaluate the health of your group:

Find out whether the group is measuring up to what members expected of it. Go back to your first meeting where members said why they came to the meeting. For an evaluation, you can ask members how well this experience measures up to their expectations.

Ask how members perceive group dynamics. Using a scale from one to ten, with ten being the highest, ask them to rate the overall participation by members of the group? On the same scale, where would they rate this group as meeting their needs? On the same scale, how would they rate the "togetherness" of this young adult group?

Ask group members to fill out an evaluation sheet on their young adult group experience. Keep the evaluation form simple. One of the simplest forms leaves plenty of blank space for responding to three requests: (1) Name the three things you want to do more of. (2) Name the three things you want to do less of. (3) Name the three things you want to keep the same.

Ask for direct feedback from one participant. Arrange ahead of time for a group member to stay a few minutes after a meeting or to meet you the next day. Ask for direct feedback about what seemed to work or not work, who seems to be participating well, who seems to be dealing with something particularly troubling, and so forth.

Give group members permission to say when they sense something is not working. As the group leader, you do not hold responsibility for the life of the group. The group's life belongs to all the members of the group. Encourage group members to take responsibility for what takes place within the group setting.

Expect and accept that, at times, discussions will fall flat, group interaction will be stilted, and group members will be grumpy. All groups have bad days. Moreover, all groups go through their own life cycles. Although your new group may take time to gel completely, you may find that after two or three sessions, one session will come when nothing seems to go right. That is normal. In fact, studies show that those groups that first show a little conflict eventually begin to move into deeper levels of relationships.

Sit back and observe. In the middle of a group discussion, sit back and try to look at the group as a whole. Does it look healthy to you? Is one person dominating? Does someone else seem to be withdrawn? How would you best describe what you observe going on within the group?

Take the "temperature" of the group. Try asking the group to take its own temperature. Would it be normal? Below normal? Feverish? What adjective would you use to describe the group's temperature?

Keep a record of evaluations. Use some form of evaluation several times during the life of the group. Compare evaluations and see how your group has changed.

✳ Making Changes

In order to sustain your young adult group, some changes may be in order. These changes may be large or small, depending on the needs of the group. You should consult the group before making any changes. Solicit their opinions and ideas.

Changing the time or day of the meeting is commonly necessary. If attendance is a problem, a better time period or new day could help. You may need to meet at a different time to accommodate the needs of one or more people. Discuss this with all group members before coming to a decision.

For one reason or another, leadership may need to change. In this situation, the current leader should be honest with the group. Give the group time to adjust. A new leader could be selected through a volunteer process or handpicked by the current leader. It is helpful if the new leader can be given some training or support from the old leader.

✳ Calling It Quits

There is a beginning and an end to everything, including young adult groups. In some cases, your group experience may have a preplanned ending at the conclusion of an eight or twelve week small group discussion. If so, the end will come as no surprise to the participants. Some will be ready to move on. Others will be sad and may have trouble letting go. Here are some suggestions on how to conclude your meetings:

If you are concluding your small group discussion or a Bible study, end the final discussion with some open-ended questions designed for closure. What was your favorite chapter and why? What did you learn about yourself and others from studying this book? How has participation in this young adult group changed you? Plan for a longer than normal discussion time. Close with a prayer giving thanks for the group and the participants.

Plan a brief social time at the conclusion of the final session. Give participants a chance to mingle, chat, and say their farewells. Have some soft drinks and snacks available. If all of the participants approve, create a list of names, phone numbers, and email addresses so participants can keep in touch. Thank the group members for their participation and for ministering to one another. Offer any observations you feel appropriate about the growth of the group and individuals.